Divided
We Fall

Anthony McGowan ✕ **Jonatronix**

OXFORD

UNIVERSITY PRESS

In this story...

Max

Cat

Ant

Tiger

The same ... or different?

Chapter 1 – A clean start

The micro-friends were in Max's garden. Rover, Ant's pet robot, was there, too. They were all supposed to be cleaning the micro-buggy. The buggy had been through lots of adventures with the children and it was very dirty.

"Do we really have to do this?" Tiger complained. "It's boring."

"The wheels are all clogged up," said Max, seriously. "We've got to keep the buggy in tip-top order. We don't want it to break down and leave us stranded somewhere, do we? It won't take long if we all work together."

"If you say so," Ant shrugged.

"So," Max continued, "could you three please go and fill up the buckets with water?"

"Yes, sir," Tiger replied, sarcastically. He didn't always like the way Max told them what to do.

"Oh, come on, Tiger," said Cat. "You never know, it might be fun."

"Carrying buckets? Fun? About as much fun as hitting yourself over the head with a fish. I'd rather be skateboarding any day."

The children climbed up some plant pots that were stacked like steps. Tiger balanced on the edge and began to fill the buckets.

"Careful up there," yelled Ant, but it was too late. Tiger fell in! Luckily he was a good swimmer and soon climbed out.

They carried the buckets back to Max.

"You're soaked," he said to Tiger. "What were you doing?"

"It was an accident," said Cat, sticking up for Tiger.

Max did not look so sure.

Max gave them all jobs. Soon each one of them was busy on a different task.

Ant cleaned the inside of the buggy. He was the smallest and so could reach into all the nooks and crannies.

Cat washed the sides, making them shine and sparkle.

Max washed
the front,
scrubbing
hard at
the mud.

Tiger had the
dirtiest job –
cleaning
the wheels.

"Tiger, you've missed a spot," said Max.

"I was just getting to that bit," said Tiger, grumpily.

Soon Tiger was bored with cleaning. He decided it was time to have some fun. He waited until Max went to get more water, and then he dipped his sponge in his bucket and threw it at Cat.

The sponge hit her right in the face.

For a moment she looked cross. Then she started to laugh. She threw her wet sponge at Tiger, but Tiger ducked and the sponge hit Ant. Soon the three friends were all throwing wet sponges at each other, laughing loudly.

Rover kept well out of the way. He didn't like water.

Max came back just in time to get hit by a bucket full of cold dirty water, thrown by Tiger. Max staggered back and fell on the buggy. Something underneath the buggy went *CLUNK!*

"Oops, sorry, Max," said Tiger. But, even though he meant it, he couldn't stop himself from laughing.

Max was furious.

"That's just stupid!" he shouted. "The buggy might be damaged now." He turned his back on the others and began to check the micro-buggy.

"Misery guts," said Tiger quietly. "Come on, Cat. Let's go and play somewhere else."

"Yeah," said Cat, "I've had enough cleaning for one day."

"We've just about finished anyway," said Ant.

Rover bleeped at them.

"What is it, Rover?" asked Ant.

Rover bleeped again, twice.

"I think he wants us to stay here," said Ant.

"You stay if you want to," said Tiger,
"but I'm off."

"Me too," said Cat.

Ant followed them, reluctantly.

As the children walked away, the little red
robot watched them. He looked worried.

Chapter 3 – Adventure playground

Cat, Ant and Tiger went down to the bottom of Max's garden. It was where Max's dad kept his garden tools along with lots of other junk from the house.

"This is fantastic," said Tiger. "Look at all this stuff!"

"Let's build an adventure playground," said Ant.

"Cool!" said the others.

The children worked together to build their playground. They built hurdles to jump over, set up spades to slide down and made a seesaw from a piece of wood balanced over an old cotton reel.

"This is the most fun we've had all day," said Cat, as she bounced up and down on an old bedspring.

Tiger looked thoughtful.

"I feel a bit mean about leaving Max to fix the buggy by himself. I'm going to go and get him. He'll love this playground."

Chapter 4 - What's wrong, Rover?

"Could somebody please pass me a spanner?"
Max called from under the buggy.

He'd been concentrating so hard on fixing the
buggy that he hadn't even realized the others
had gone. When no one answered, he slid out.
Rover was waiting for him.

"I wonder where the others have got to?"
he said. He was sorry that he'd shouted at
his friends.

Rover bleeped loudly.

"What's wrong, Rover? You don't sound very happy."

Rover took Max's hand gently and pulled him.

"What's the matter?" Suddenly Max felt worried. "You want me to follow you?"

Rover tried again to pull him in the direction the others had gone.

"I've got a better idea," Max said.

Chapter 5 – Some new friends?

Tiger was about to go and get Max when he noticed something in the bushes.

"Hey, is that Rover over there?" he said.

It certainly looked like the friendly little robot.

"What are you hiding for, Rover?" asked Cat.

Ant peered at the shiny red robot, half
hidden in the leaves.

"Wait a minute," he said, "I'm not sure ..."

Just then, another red robot appeared next to
the first.

"Hang on, there are *two* Rovers," said Tiger.
"He must have found a friend. How cool is
that? Let's go and play with them."

Tiger began to walk towards the robots.

"Be careful," warned Cat, "I've got a bad feeling about this."

"Don't be daft," cried Tiger, over his shoulder. "Rover's harmless, isn't he? His friends must be too."

When he had almost reached them, he noticed a third robot.

And then a fourth …

started to laugh but then he noticed
ese robots didn't look as friendly as
er after all. There was a wicked glint in
eir eyes. He was completely surrounded.

The four robots jumped towards Tiger.
They pinned his arms and legs to the ground.
He couldn't move. Then one of the robots
stretched out its pincers, ready to snip the
watch from Tiger's wrist.

"Help!" shouted Tiger.

"They're after your watch," yelled Cat.

"What shall we do?" cried Ant.

"They're too strong," shouted Tiger. "Go and get Max!"

Cat and Ant looked at each other in horror.

Aaaaarghhhh!

Chapter 6 – Max to the rescue

Suddenly there was a roar and a *CRASH!*

It was Max in the micro-buggy. He smashed into the robot that was snapping its pincers at Tiger, then swerved out of the way. The robot went flying. The other three quickly backed away.

Max skidded to a halt.

"Quick!" he yelled. "Jump in."

Cat and Ant helped Tiger into the buggy.

"What's going on?" said Max. "Where have all these other Rovers come from?"

Before they could answer, Ant noticed that the robots were scuttling towards the micro-buggy.

"No time for explanations," he yelled. "Go, go, go!"

Max revved the engine and the micro-buggy zoomed off.

They zipped through the grass, swerved round stones and skidded in the mud. Tiger's clean wheels got dirty again and, as the mud stuck to the wheels, the buggy began to slow.

"Oh, no!" cried Tiger. "They're gaining on us!"

A robot clutched at the side of the buggy with its strong metal jaws.

"It's got us!" yelled Ant.

Max tried to make the buggy go faster but the wheels were now so clogged with mud that they did not pick up any speed. Max changed direction. He steered straight into a puddle.

"What are you doing?" cried Cat.

"Trust me!" said Max.

The buggy splashed through the puddle. As the wheels spun round, the mud was washed off. Dirty water splashed all over the robots. Then the piece of the buggy that the robot was hanging on to snapped off, and the robot fell back into the puddle.

They were free! They zoomed off again.

The robots were left splattered and stuck in the mud.

"That was *way* too close," said Ant.

"We're really sorry, Max," said Cat. "Thanks for rescuing us. How did you know we were in trouble?"

"It was Rover. He seemed to know that those other robots were around."

"I wonder what they were after?" said Ant.

"They were after my watch!" snorted Tiger.

"But where did they come from?" said Cat.

"I don't know," said Max. He thought back to the note that had been with the watches when they had found them: *Keep us secret. Keep us safe.* "This changes everything," he continued. "If someone's trying to get the watches, it means we've got to work together as a team to keep them safe."

The others nodded.

"So I'm going to start by saying sorry for shouting at you earlier," said Max. "And you know what?"

"What?" said the others together.

"One of the things teams have to do together is have fun. Who wants to drive the buggy?"

To find out more about teamwork read ...

Let's form a Band!

To find out more about the robots and where they came from read ...

A NASTI Surprise

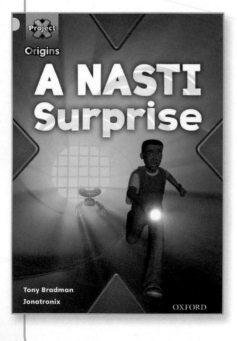

After reading

Talk with your child about the book. Here are some questions you could ask:

- Why did Cat, Ant and Tiger leave Max by himself? Were they right to do this? What happened as a result?
- Why did Tiger think it was safe to go up to the new robots?
- What were the new robots after?
- Did you like this book? Why or why not?

Encourage your child to read the story again. This will build their reading confidence and reading fluency.

Other things to do

Keep talking about this book. If your child wants to, they could write or draw their own story about meeting a robot. Or they could draw and label a diagram of the new robot – use page 3 to help.

OXFORD
UNIVERSITY PRESS

Great Clarendon Street, Oxford, OX2 6DP, United Kingdom

Oxford University Press is a department of the University of Oxford.
It furthers the University's objective of excellence in research, scholarship,
and education by publishing worldwide. Oxford is a registered trade mark of
Oxford University Press in the UK and in certain other countries

© Oxford University Press 2009

The moral rights of the author, Anthony McGowan, have been asserted.

First Edition published in 2009
This Edition published in 2014

British Library Cataloguing in Publication Data
Data available

978-0-19-830226-1

9 10 8

Paper used in the production of this book is a natural, recyclable product
made from wood grown in sustainable forests. The manufacturing process conforms
to the environmental regulations of the country of origin.

Printed in China by Leo Paper Products Ltd

Acknowledgements

Illustrations by Jonatronix Ltd
Project X concept by Rod Theodorou and Emma Lynch
Lead Author of the Project X character books: Tony Bradman

Origins

Book Band 10
White

Oxford
Level 10

Letters and Sounds
Phase 6

Divided We Fall

Tiger, Cat and Ant leave Max
to clean the micro-buggy by himself.
They soon begin to regret it when
they are chased by some
unfriendly robots.

Great for Guided Reading

Titles on the theme: *Working as a Team*

The Balloon Team (Fiction)

> **Divided We Fall** (Fiction)

Fee Fie Fo ... Mum! (Fiction)

Let's Form a Band! (Non-fiction)

The Beautiful Team (Non-fiction)

OXFORD
UNIVERSITY PRESS

How to get in touch:
web   www.oxfordprimary.co.uk
email   schools.enquiries.uk@oup.com
tel.   +44 (0) 1536 452610
fax   +44 (0) 1865 313472

ISBN 978-0-19

9 780198 30

KQ-858-248

www.lettsrevise.com

Need to spice up your revision a bit?

Find out which subjects you'll blast through and which need a bit more work with our fast and furious quick fire quiz created especially for GCSE students.

But don't just try once – we have thousands of questions on our database, so you can keep on playing, and exercise those little grey cells.

You'll need them in peak condition to get the result you want in your GCSE exams!

**www.lettsrevise.com –
Give Yourself the Edge!**

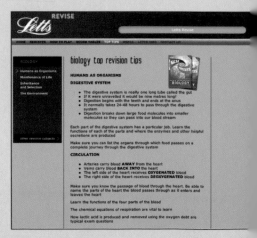